Holy Communion is...

Holy Communion is...

Thirteen Communion Messages

R. E. LYBRAND

C.S.S. Publishing Co., Inc.
Lima, Ohio

HOLY COMMUNION IS . . .

Copyright © 1987 by
The C.S.S. Publishing Company, Inc.
Lima, Ohio

All rights reserved. No part of this publication may be reproduced, stored in a retrieval system, or transmitted in any form or by any means, electronic, mechanical, photocopying, recording, or otherwise, without the prior permission of the publisher. Inquiries should be addressed to: The C.S.S. Publishing Company, Inc., 628 South Main Street, Lima, Ohio 45804.

Library of Congress Cataloging-in-Publication Data

Lybrand, R. E., 1949-
    Holy Communion is —.

    1. Communion sermons.   2. Sermons, American.   I. Title.
BV4257.5.L93   1987   252'.6   86-28345
ISBN 0-89536-853-6

7812 / ISBN 0-89536-853-6   PRINTED IN U.S.A.

This book is dedicated to
my Family in Christ at Grace Church
with whom I regularly celebrate
the Lord's Presence in Holy Communion.

Table of Contents

Foreword		8
Preface		9
	Holy Communion Is . . .	
1. January	. . . **Real Presence**	11
2. February	. . . **Remembering**	16
3. March	. . . **Refreshment**	21
4. April	. . . **Realizing Forgiveness**	25
5. May	. . . **Relief**	30
6. June	. . . **Reconciliation**	37
7. July	. . . **Response to an Invitation**	42
8. August	. . . **Repentance**	48
9. September	. . . **Remedial**	53
10. October	. . . **Reunion**	58
11. November	. . . **Reformed**	63
12. December	. . . **Rejoicing in His Coming**	68
13. First Communion Sunday	. . . **Running No More**	74

Foreword

These sermons are written by a pastor who is deeply concerned for his people and devotionally committed to the Word of God.

They are written with a keen awareness of the needs of the person in the pew and at the same time reflect the response of God's Word to meet these needs with the comfort of God's powerful presence and forgiving grace.

On Saturday night busy pastors will find in this series of sermons the oil of helpful insights, fresh images and usable illustrations to keep their midnight lamps burning brightly as they prepare the sermon for Sunday morning.

> Richard Carl Hoefler
> Professor of Preaching and Worship
> Lutheran Theological Southern Seminary
> Columbia, South Carolina

Preface

Special foods are often associated with unique celebrations. If the table were adorned with turkey, dressing, cranberry sauce, and all the trimmings, without a doubt it would be Thanksgiving dinner. When we see a beautifully decorated cake aglow with candles and side dishes of ice cream, everyone knows it is a birthday celebration. Readily we associate cherry pie with George Washington's birthday. And of course, when a pastor mentions a meal of bread and wine, every Christian associates that menu with the Lord's Supper.

Even though most all Christians know *what* will be served in Holy Communion, *how* it will be given, and the customary *manner* of receiving it, many do not understand the deeper meanings of this sacramental meal. In this volume of sermons, I have addressed some basic questions which are of interest to the worshiper in the pew. Having heard a politician pound his fist and insist that our state's educational system must get back to teaching the basic "R's" — Reading, Riting, and Rithmetic (and obviously a course is also needed in spelling) — I decided that we can better understand communion with some basic "R" words too.

Each chapter is a sermon about some aspect of the Lord's Supper. Although I tried to write from a position of clear Biblical theology, there is no escaping the fact that I read the Scriptures through Lutheran glasses. My prayer is that the theological position not be a hindrance to your allowing the Holy Spirit to speak to your heart and mind. Whether you refer to communion as a sacrament or an ordinance is irrelevant. It is still the Lord's meal. It is he who is the host. It is Christ who meets us with love, forgiveness, and strength as we humbly dine with him at his meal of Grace.

Pastors, I hope the simple thoughts, structures, and gimmicks of the sermons will help you proclaim the Lord's presence and power. Although the sermons are assigned to particular months in the Table of Contents, most of them can be used in any season of the Church Year with a few minor revisions. Please use them in any way that will help your congregation experience the presence of the Risen Lord. Be assured that they came from the pen of one who has a genuine love for the Lord and a sincere desire to be true to his Word.

I am indeed grateful to many people for their help in this project: the congregation of Grace Lutheran for giving me the concentrated study time which I find essential for such a series; my generous friends, John and June Connor, for the use of their "retreat" in which I read and wrote;

Debby Wood, the intern at Grace Church who helped me with more inclusive language; Michelle Sapp for typing the manuscript; and my dear, supportive wife Jackie and my children, Mauri and Brett, for their patient endurance as I worked. May God bless you as you read and proclaim!

R. E. L.

1 | Communion Is
Real Presence

John 1:1-14

In the beginning was the Word, and the Word was with God, and the Word was God. He was in the beginning with God; all things were made through him, and without him was not anything made that was made. In him was life, and the life was the light of men. The light shines in the darkness, and the darkness has not overcome it. There was a man sent from God, whose name was John. He came for testimony, to bear witness to the light, that all might believe through him. He was not the light, but came to bear witness to the light. The true light that enlightens every man was coming into the world. He was in the world, and the world was made through him, yet the world knew him not. He came to his own home, and his own people received him not. But to all who received him, who believed in his name, he gave power to become children of God; who were born, not of blood nor of the will of the flesh nor of the will of man, but of God. And the Word became flesh and dwelt among us, full of grace and truth; we have beheld his glory, glory as of the only Son from the Father.

It is said that King Charles V, the king of Scotland, many years ago, wondered what life was like for the people of his kingdom. In a desire to better know them and to more graciously govern them, he would occasionally exchange his royal robes for common clothes and walk from his lofty palace into the soiled streets. Completely disguised as a commoner, he walked through the market place, worked in the fields and ate at the tables of his peasant people. All of that was done by King Charles in an attempt to better understand and more fully identify with the people of his kingdom. But what he did partially and imperfectly, God did completely and perfectly. In Jesus Christ, God became human and lived on this earth. He did not come to learn more about us and to identify with us. He came to help us know and identify with Him.

We read about the glorious incarnation in the Gospel of John. The first verse of the first chapter says: "In the beginning was the Word, and the Word was with God and the Word was God." Then in verse 14 we find out what God did: "And the Word became flesh and lived among us . . ." You see, God became a human being in Jesus, the Christ. The same event is described by the Apostle Paul in Philippians 2 where he wrote about Christ who "humbled himself, taking the very nature of a servant and came in human likeness. And being found in appearance as a man, He humbled himself and became obedient unto death . . ."

The incarnation is central to our celebration of this Christmas Season. It is central to our Faith, to believe that in Jesus, God stepped down from heaven, and became completely immersed in the life of humanity. It was such a perfect incarnation that the Church for centuries has called Jesus "true God and true man." Many will ask how it is possible for Jesus to be completely human and completely divine at the same time — that is not logical or reasonable! The Church then replies as did Martin Luther, that no one can understand or adequately explain the natures of Christ because it is simply one of the great mysteries of our faith. It is something that Scripture affirms as true while we simply stand in awe, trying to illustrate it and symbolize it, even though we cannot explain it. But we believe that Jesus of Nazareth was, at the same time, fully human and fully divine.

Now, when some people read the Gospel narratives, they try to divide the events of our Lord's ministry, concluding that there were certain times when Jesus was acting according to his Divine nature — such as when he healed the sick, cast out demons, raised the dead, and walked on the water — and there were other times when Christ's humanity was dominant — such as when he wept at the tomb of Lazarus, prayed in the Garden of Gethsemane, angrily cast out the money changers from the temple, and when he slept, ate and rested his body. But such a dissecting of our Lord's humanity and divinity is both inadequate and inaccurate. Dr. Fred Schott of Southern Seminary used to illustrate this heretical practice by gluing two boards together. On one board was written "Divine Nature" and on the other board were the words "Human Nature." Those who hold to this view believe that Jesus sometimes acted divine and other times acted human as he "flip-flopped" between his two natures. But we Christians believe that Jesus was, at the same time, human and divine. In all that he did, the two natures participated fully. The humanity and divinity were totally and completely inseparable in Jesus. Perhaps the inseparability of Christ's two natures could be illustrated with a glass of water and a cup of sugar. The two substances are distinct and different in appearance. But when the sugar is dissolved in the water, they become one. The sweetness of the sugar completely permeates the water. We should never push an illustration too far, but this is a helpful example of how the two natures of Christ completely permeate each other. Jesus was totally human and totally divine; one could not be separated from the other. In him, God became flesh and lived among us in order to be fully revealed to us.

Now in the same mysterious way that God became flesh and entered the world in Jesus, we Lutherans believe that our Lord comes into our midst and into our lives in Holy Communion. We believe that Christ is really present "in, with, and under" these elements of bread and wine. What God did in a cosmic sense on the first Christmas by coming into the World, he does in an individual sense in Holy Communion by coming to you and me! And in the same way that the two natures of Christ were inseparable, the body and blood of Christ are inseparable from the bread and wine. We don't believe we can look at the bread under a microscope and see molecules of Christ's flesh. We don't believe that the wine actually changes into Christ's blood. But we do believe that Christ is present in Holy Communion.

As Martin Luther wrote: "We are . . . not so mad as to believe that Christ's body is in the bread in a manner as crude and visible as bread is in a basket or wine in a cup . . . . We do, however, unhesitatingly believe that His body is there, as His words 'This is my body' indicate . . . . He is where the bread is . . ." (*What Luther Says*, Vol. II., p. 796) We believe that Christ is really present when we eat the bread and drink the wine of Holy Communion. This is not something we can explain but something we can experience. When we go to the altar with repentant hearts and humble faith, we experience the mysterious and powerful presence of Christ. He comes to each of us individually — and personally. Christ is present to relieve our hearts of the tremendous load of guilt for which we need forgiveness. The Lord is present to strengthen us to overcome our temptations and weaknesses. He is present to lift from our shoulders the weight of our worries and fears. Jesus is present to assure us that no matter what has happened or will happen, we will be all right because he is always with us.

Several years ago a beautiful story appeared in the "Bible Expositor and Illuminator." It was about a Christian man whose wife was killed in a tragic automobile accident leaving him to care for their three-year-old daughter. All the joy he had known seemed to vanish in his grief. The night after the funeral, he was preparing his daughter for bed when the lights went out all over the house. His little girl became afraid so he held her right in his arms. At first she snuggled against him in silence, but when her fears subsided she said, "It's so dark! But I'm not afraid daddy because you are here with me!" Tears welled up in the father's eyes. He buried his face in his daughter's hair and reflected on what she had said, saying: "Yes dear, my life is dark right now. But I'm not afraid either, because I know that my Heavenly Father is with me too." That man received courage and comfort from knowing that God was with him.

That same comforting reassurance is ours today. No matter how dark your life is right now . . . No matter what struggles and troubles you are having to endure, I want you to rest assured in the knowledge that Christ is really present with you today through these elements of bread and wine. As you go to the communion table, Christ will come to you in mystery and power. Don't try to explain his presence, just experience it. Experience the cleansing power of his forgiveness, offering you newness of life. Experience the reassurance of Christ's constant presence, not only at this altar but in your daily life with him. Experience the warm embrace of his loving arms and know that you will be all right because Christ is with you.

2 | Communion Is **Remembering**

Luke 22:14-19

And when the hour came, he sat at table, and the apostles with him. And he said to them, "I have earnestly desired to eat this passover with you before I suffer; for I tell you I shall not eat it until it is fulfilled in the kingdom of God." And he took a cup, and when he had given thanks he said, "Take this, and divide it among yourselves; for I tell you that from now on I shall not drink of the fruit of the vine until the kingdom of God comes." And he took bread, and when he had given thanks he broke it and gave it to them, saying, "This is my body."

In Norway, there is a small church called the Church of the Lamb. Instead of having a cross on its steeple, it has the figure of a lamb. The people of that village love to tell why that lamb was placed on the top of their church. One day, as work was being completed on the brand new church building, a young man lost his footing and slipped from the steeple. At the precise moment that he was falling toward the ground, a flock of sheep was passing by. The workman fell right on top of a little lamb. The man's life was saved as the lamb was crushed to death. Today, when the townspeople see that lamb on top of the steeple, they remember how its life was sacrificed to save the life of that construction worker. But more importantly, they are reminded of Jesus, the Lamb of God, who willingly, not accidentally, laid down his life to save all people.

This morning, even though we do not have a lamb on our church steeple, we do have the elements of Communion on our altar. The bread and wine help us remember the atoning, redeeming, saving work of the Lamb of God on the Cross of Calvary. One of the primary reasons we eat the bread and wine of Holy Communion is to remember, for Jesus said, "Do this in remembrance of Me."

Of course we do not believe that Holy Communion is only a memorial service, there is much more to it than that. We believe that in some mysterious, unexplainable way, Jesus Christ himself is really present, calling us to remember. And what is it that our Lord wants us to remember? First, he wants us to remember his redeeming sacrifice for us! When Jesus died, more happened than just another Jew being hanged on a Roman Cross. Something of cosmic and eternal importance took place, and we must never forget that. In Jesus, our wondrous God came to earth and lived in perfect obedience to his own will and Law. Christ lived in complete harmony and fellowship with God. He identified fully with humanity in every way except one — he did not sin. In Hebrews 4:15 we read ". . . we have (a high priest) who has been tempted in every way that we have been tempted, yet he did not sin." Since Jesus did not sin, but lived in perfect obedience to the will of God, he did not deserve to die. For we read in Romans 6:23 that "the wages of sin is death." Since Christ did not sin, he did not deserve sin's wages — death. He had no sins to be punished for but willingly went to the cross to receive the punishment of death because of your sin and mine. Jesus accepted our punishment so we might be set free from it. We sinned and he took our punishment . . . he died so we wouldn't have to. So . . . because of Jesus you and I don't have to live in fear of eternal death. Jesus Christ willingly accepted a punishment that he did not deserve in order to give us the gift of eternal life that we do not deserve. We must never forget what our Lord has done for us. We should daily remember his loving sacrifice! When we touch the bread and taste the wine, it helps us remember his body broken and his blood poured out for us.

One day a little girl asked her father why he always carried a little piece of flat metal in his pocket. Her father smiled warmly, sat down with his daughter and began to explain, "Honey, during World War II my company was under heavy attack. The fighting was fierce! I was in a fox hole with four of my closest buddies. All of a sudden a hand grenade came tumbling in. All of us would have been killed had it not been for Tom. He threw himself onto that grenade and absorbed the explosion with his body. Tom gave his life for his friends. From that day to this I have carried his dog tags in my pocket. Whenever I touch them, I remember his loving sacrifice for me, how he died so I might live.

My fellow believers, in a very similar way, when we feel the bread of Holy Communion in our hands and taste the wine on our lips, we should remember the sacrificial death of our Lord Jesus Christ — how he died so we might live, how he suffered the penalty and punishment of our sins so that we would be set free for abundant life today and eternal life tomorrow. Holy Communion helps us remember Christ's redeeming sacrifice for us.

Not only do we remember the redemption that Christ's death accomplished, but we should also remember that his death demonstrated his enormous love for each of us. In John 15:13 Jesus said, "Greater love has no man than this, that a man lay down his life for his friends." Is there anybody who would die for you? Is there anyone whom you would die for? Christ willingly laid down his life for you and me — his friends.

Christ's death was not accidental as it was for the lamb on the steeple. His death was not the result of irreversible circumstances set in motion by the scheming of clever enemies. His death was the intentional action of a Gracious God. It was Christ's willing choice to demonstrate his love for you and me. Jesus said in John 10:17-18, "In this reason the Father loves me, because I lay down my life . . . No one takes it from me, but I lay it down of my own accord." Christ willingly endured the agonizing death on the cross in order to show you and me and all people how much he loves us. And he wasn't dying for good people but those who disobeyed, rebelled, those who did not believe or love him. Christ died for sinners! In Romans 5:8, the apostle Paul wrote: "But God shows his love for us in that while we were yet sinners, Christ died for us." Sacrifice! What a demonstration that is of love!

There is a true and touching story about two little children who did not know each other even though they attended the same school. The only thing they had in common was a very rare blood type. One of the youngsters, named Charlie, was in the hospital with an unusual disease and was very near death. His only chance for survival was to have a complete blood transfusion. His blood type was so rare that only one possible donor could be found: ten year old Tammy. The doctors went to Tammy and explained the situation and said, "Tammy, are you willing to give your blood to Charlie so he can live?" Then they gave her a while to think it over. The girl hesitated — her lower lip began to tremble — finally she smiled and said, "All right, I'll give my blood to Charlie because I think that's what Jesus would want me to do." That afternoon the two children lay side by side in a sterile hospital room. Neither said a word as they watched Tammy's blood flow slowly through the tube into Charlie's vein. The ordeal was almost over when the silence was broken by Tammy who said softly, "Say doctor, how much longer will it be before I die?" It was then that the doctor realized what a tremendous sacrifice Tammy had been willing to make. She actually thought that in giving her blood to her dying school mate, she was giving up her life.

Jesus must have been very proud of that young Christian who was willing to demonstrate her love by laying down her life for another. When we drink the wine of Holy Communion, we are reminded of Christ's blood being poured out for us. We remember his sacrificial death on the Cross — the death to end eternal death for all who believe in him. And we see on the cross, the greatest demonstration of God's love for us. Remember what Romans 5:8 says, "But God shows his love for us in that while we were yet sinners, Christ died for us." What a costly, painful way for God to say, "I love you."

When you come to the altar to drink the wine and eat the bread of Holy Communion today, it should remind you of God's tremendous love for you. When you feel the bread, taste the wine, I hope you will remember . . . remember the lamb who died on the Cross so you might live; remember the lamb who laid down his life just to say, "I love you, my child"; remember the lamb who is with you to forgive, to heal, to strengthen and to restore; remember the Lamb of God.

3 | Communion Is **Refreshment**

Mark 14:22-26

And as they were eating, he took bread, and blessed, and broke it, and gave it to them, and said, "Take; this is my body." And he took a cup, and when he had given thanks he gave it to them, and they all drank of it. And he said to them, "This is my blood of the covenant, which is poured out for many. Truly, I say to you, I shall not drink again of the fruit of the vine until that day when I drink it new in the kingdom of God." And when they had sung a hymn, they went out to the Mount of Olives.

John 19:28-30

After this Jesus, knowing that all was now finished, said (to fulfil the scripture), "I thirst." A bowl full of vinegar stood there; so they put a sponge full of the vinegar on hyssop and held it to his mouth. When Jesus had received the vinegar, he said, "It is finished"; and he bowed his head and gave up his spirit.

Death by crucifixion was such an agonizing way to die. The dehydration which came before death was especially severe. So we can be sure that all the humanity of Jesus was screaming forth as he said "I thirst." Without question, Jesus was severely thirsty as he hung upon the cross. His cry for a drink is quite normal — very human indeed. It was a cry for something wet to moisten his cracked lips and soothe his parched throat.

In Palestine during the afternoon, a warm and oftentimes a scorchingly hot wind blows in from the desert. The heat it generates can wither vegetation when it is at its worst. It always sent people running for shade and cover . . . no one remained in the open with no protection — unless of course it was a tragic figure slumped on a cross on a shadeless hill. As you remember, Jesus was pinned to that cross in the morning hours of Good Friday. Before that, he had been beaten with a whip at the order of Pilate. He had been kept awake all night with questions and humiliating trials, making it nearly forty-eight hours that he went without rest. After that, he had to drag a cross up the hilly streets of Jerusalem and out beyond its walls to a hill named Golgotha. Arriving at his destination, Jesus was laid down on the wood plank and nailed fast. Finally, he was lifted up, in front of the jeering crowd — exhausted, bruised, aching, and thirsty. With the focused rays of the boiling hot sun, he reached the point where he needed help coping with the anguish of his fevered body. So he called out for some compassion. What the Lord wanted was for some merciful person standing within range of his voice to give him a refreshing drink to soothe his parched lips. Jesus cried out, "I thirst."

How can anyone hear these two words from the cross and not feel the great intensity of his suffering? Too many times we think that Jesus really did not suffer much because he was divine. But we must remember the mystery that he was also just as human as we are. He suffered as much as we would have. Have you ever gotten a thorn in your finger while walking in the woods or in a rose garden? Then you can imagine how painful it would be to have hundreds of thorns smashed down onto your head. Jesus suffered that for us. Have you ever stepped on a nail as a child while walking barefoot? Or have you ever stuck a splinter into your hand? Then multiply that pain 1000 times and you'll be able to imagine the pain Jesus felt when those spikes were pounded through his hands and feet. The Lord suffered that for us. Have you ever accidentally sliced your finger with a knife and cried because of the pain? Well imagine how it was for Jesus when that whip lacerated his back. The Lord suffered that pain for us! Have you ever been thirsty? Can you imagine what it would be like to go for hours without drinking anything and then hang on a cross in the blazing sun with the desert wind parching your skin? Jesus endured that for us.

We must never forget all that the Lord went through to redeem us from Satan's power and offer us forgiveness and salvation. We must never forget. To help us remember, our Lord instituted a special meal on this very night nearly 2000 years ago. It is a simple meal of bread and wine but it has a powerful effect in the Christian's life. On Thursday night, after Jesus and the Apostles had finished the Passover Meal, the Lord took a piece of bread from the table and broke it — saying that it was his Body which would be broken with our sins. Then he instructed his followers to eat it in remembrance of the pain he endured for us on the cross. After that Jesus took the cup of wine and said that it was his blood which would be poured out for the forgiveness of our sins. Then he instructed all his followers to drink from that cup of wine in remembrance of the painful, agonizing way his blood was poured out for our salvation. So often we forget what Christ has done for us. So often we wander away from close fellowship with him. That's one reason he gave us Holy Communion — to remind us of all he has done — all the pain he has endured.

A wife who had been unfaithful to her husband decided to get a divorce so she left him. A few weeks later, she mailed him a letter requesting that all her things be sent to her new apartment. He still loved his unfaithful wife and was very sad as he gathered her things together and packed them in a trunk. Before closing the lid, he placed a few keepsakes on top: her diamond ring that she had thrown in the trash, an album of their wedding pictures, and a small plastic box containing the little shoes of their baby who had died. When the wife opened the trunk and saw those things on top, her heart was broken. The memory of all the love and joy she once had with her husband came flooding back into her mind. Shedding bitter tears of repentance, she acknowledged her sin and unfaithfulness, and was reconciled to her husband.

    Likewise our Lord has given us some special keepsakes, some special symbols to remind us of his love. Knowing the unfaithfulness of our hearts and how easy it is for us to forget him, Jesus instituted this special supper to be a reminder of his sacrifice for us. The breaking of this bread symbolized the breaking of his Body by our sin. The outpouring of this wine symbolized the spilling of his Blood for our forgiveness. Christ thirsted because of his agonizing ordeal on the Cross for us. And now Christ invites you to come to his Table if you are thirsting for a closer relationship with him . . . Come if you are thirsting for a new start in life . . . come if you are thirsting for forgiveness of your Sin. . . Come with repentant hearts if you are thirsting for the Lord who thirsted for you . . . Come receive refreshment for your sin-shattered life.

4 | Communion Is
Realizing Forgiveness

Matthew 26:27-29

And he took a cup, and when he had given thanks he gave it to them, saying, "Drink of it, all of you; for this is my blood of the covenant, which is poured out for many for the forgiveness of sins. I tell you I shall not drink again of this fruit of the vine until that day when I drink it new with you in my Father's kingdom."

How do you normally react when someone offends you in some way? Perhaps they do something to embarrass you in public. Or maybe they humiliate you in front of your friends. How do you respond when someone swindles you out of money or sells you something that turns out to be worthless? All too often our human reaction to such situations is to seek revenge! We begin plotting ways to even the score, to get them back for what they did to us. This, all too human way of reacting, was illustrated for me this summer at the beach when I saw a young lady wearing a T-shirt which said, "I don't get mad . . . I get even."

You see, some people pride themselves in their skill for getting revenge . . . in their ability to be one up on the next person . . . to always have the last word or a cutting comeback. But one of the best stories of revenge I've seen is one I read not long ago:

There was a quiet truck driver hauling a load across country. Late one evening, he stopped at a roadside diner for supper. As he was eating, three rather rough-looking motorcyclists roared-up to the diner's entrance. All eyes were upon them as they strolled into the dining room wearing dirty leather jackets. For some reason, they selected the quiet truck driver as the target for their hatefulness. Walking over to his table, the motorcyclists began laughing at him and cursing him. One of them poured salt and pepper over his head. Another threw his pie onto the floor and smashed it with his boot. The third dumped a cup of coffee into his lap. After all that abuse, the trucker got up from his table without uttering a word. He calmly paid his bill and left the diner. The motorcyclists made fun of him as he left. One of them said, "He's the biggest coward I've ever seen. He sure ain't much of a fighter." The cashier behind the counter peered through the window and replied, "No, he ain't much of a driver either. He just drove his truck over three motorcycles out in the parking lot."

That's what we might call "Instant Revenge." And there is something in us that rejoices in the quick thinking of that truck driver because we conclude that somehow he redeemed himself from that embarrassing situation. He got even! We wish we could be so clever and quick thinking to always even the score when someone "gets one on us." In this worldly society, we think we must be skillful and astute in our ability to get revenge because we know that most often that's the way it is in human relationships. When we hurt or anger someone, even by accident, we fully expect that someday, somehow, the person will get us back.

Because of our frequent experience of vengeance in our human relationships, there is little wonder that we have projected those expectations into our divine relationship with God. We know how vengeful we become when someone offends us. We know how vengeful others become when we wrong them. So we conclude that God will seek vengeance upon us when we do wrong or offend him in some way. Unfortunately, too many of us perceive God to operate like a vengeful Santa Claus in the sky: "He's making a list and checking it twice... gonna find out who's naughty and nice." And once God discovers how naughty we really are — how unfaithful we've been — he'll get us... in his desire for revenge, in his desire to get even with us.

How often I have sat with persons whose lives have been touched by tragedy. Almost inevitably they will ask, "Why is God punishing me like this?" Their conclusion is that the tragedy they endured was God's way of getting revenge for their sins. It was God's way of evening the score. There was a member of a congregation whose twelve year old son died of leukemia. He honestly believed that God killed his son to punish him for not being faithful to the church. So many sincere Christians today have what I call a "Maude Finley theology." Like that TV character said so often, if you do something wrong, "God will get you for that."

But this is merely a projection of human ways into God's ways. Jesus showed us so clearly and beautifully that God does not deal with us that way under the New Covenant. God does not treat us the way we treat each other. We can see an example of this in Luke 9:52ff. One day Jesus and his disciples were going through a Samaritan village on their way toward Jerusalem. Now remember, there was mutual hatred between Jews and Samaritans. The townspeople would not permit them to travel through their village because they were Jews heading to Jerusalem. In anger James and John said, "Lord, do you want us to call fire down from heaven to destroy them?" A very human and vengeful reaction. But Jesus sternly rebuked them for their desire for revenge. Why the stern rebuke? Because Jesus knew God's ways are different from human ways. Jesus wasn't vengeful. He simply took another road to Jerusalem.

When we offend God with our sinful, rebellious, living, He does not seek vengeance upon us. The Almighty's vengeful wrath was unleashed upon the sins of humanity when Christ became sin on the cross. With all the sins of the world on his shoulders, Christ died an agonizing death in order to receive the punishment that you and I deserve . . . in order to accept the vengeful wrath on our behalf. Christ paid the penalty of our sin; therefore God is no longer seeking to even the score. He is no longer seeking vengeance. Now he's seeking to help us realize forgiveness! Let me illustrate: An elderly pastor was watching several children play in his yard when he noticed one of them with a BB gun pointed toward his livingroom window. The next thing he heard was the shattering of glass; then all the children ran away. Pastor Jamison had the window replaced the very next day. It wasn't long before he learned the identity of the child who had pulled the trigger — his name was Dave White. As time passed the other children drifted back to play in the yard again, but Dave stayed away. When asked why, the others said Dave was afraid that Pastor Jamison was angry and would hurt him if he returned. One day while in a store, the pastor saw Dave and greeted him in a friendly manner saying, "Dave, I paid for the window and as far as I'm concerned everything is all right. Come on back and play with your friends." But it was several weeks before the youngster got the courage to come back. He heard Pastor Jamison say that everything was all right — but somehow he still wasn't sure.

One afternoon while the children were playing, the old man came outside with cookies and Kool-Aid for them all. Dave stood back as though the refreshments weren't for him. The pastor said, "Come on Dave, these are for you too." It was then the boy realized that what Pastor Jamison had said was true . . . everything was all right.

You know, Holy Communion serves a similar function for us children of God. Time and again we hear God's Word telling us that we are forgiven, but for some reason we doubt it; we don't believe it! For some reason we still think God wants revenge. So to reinforce his Word — to help us realize his forgiveness, our Living, Loving Lord comes into our midst bringing us, not cookies and Kool-Aid, but bread and wine. But more happens than the mere quenching of thirst and hunger — we receive refreshments for our heart and soul. The bread reminds us of Christ's body — beaten, pierced and broken for us. The wine reminds us of Christ's blood — spilled and poured out on the cross for one purpose — that you and I might be forgiven and reconciled to God.

Maybe you haven't shattered a window in God's house, but perhaps you've broken God's heart by your lack of faithfulness in worship and in the study of his Word. Confess that to God, then come to Holy Communion and realize that he has forgiven you. Have you thrust that spear more deeply into Christ's side by your apathy toward the hurting and hungry in this world? Acknowledge that to God, then come to his table and realize that you are forgiven. Have you shattered God's will through the way you treat your family or the way you conduct your life when no one sees or hears the secret thoughts and desires you entertain in your mind? Confess those to God, then come to his table and realize that you are forgiven.

We live in the painful reality that all of us are sinners. We all fall short of God's glory and expectations of us as his children. Too many of us fully expect God to get us — to get even — to vent the pain in his heart onto our lives with vengeful wrath — after all, that is the way we so often treat others and are treated by them. But this morning, God invites us to a special meal of bread and wine where he will meet us to remind us not of his vengeful wrath but his forgiving love. To remind us that when Jesus Christ died, it was so we could be forgiven: "This cup is the New Covenant in My blood which was poured out for you and all people for the forgiveness of sin." When you rise from the Lord's table today, I hope you will feel refreshed. I hope you will realize that you are fully forgiven and free to start life again . . . free from the past. I hope you will realize you are forgiven.

5 | Communion Is
Relief

Matthew 11:28-30

Come to me, all who labor and are heavy laden, and I will give you rest. Take my yoke upon you, and learn from me; for I am gentle and lowly in heart, and you will find rest for your souls. For my yoke is easy, and my burden is light.

I'm worried about education in America. My concern right now is different from the usual ones about drug abuse, sexual immorality and secularistic ideas. I'm worried about the way some Americans have learned to spell. There are people who cannot spell even the simplest words. Perhaps you've seen that commercial on TV in which a reporter interviews several people by asking them the question: "How do you spell Relief?" Now I thought I knew how to spell relief. But evidently I don't because every single person that reporter questions spells relief, R-O-L-A-I-D-S. I've heard about the New Math — I suppose that's the New English.

I've often thought about what I would say if such a reporter asked me, "How do you spell relief?" I would say "J-E-S-U-S." Perhaps Rolaids can give physical relief but Jesus can give Spiritual relief. Rolaids might comfort a painful stomach but Jesus can comfort a broken heart. Rolaids may have the ability to calm a gaseous tummy, but Jesus has the power to calm a troubled soul. How would I spell Relief? — "J-E-S-U-S."

We Christians believe that Jesus is with us today in a very

special way. We believe that he is really present in the Sacrament of the Altar. In the bread and wine of Holy Communion Jesus comes to us, who truly believe, and gives relief for our troubled hearts and spirits. Let me briefly share with you two ways that Jesus gives relief.

First of all, Jesus gives us relief from sin and guilt. In Romans 3:23 we read that "All have sinned and fallen short of the Glory of God." There is no doubt about that, is there? Despite the fact that we are Saints because of our faith in Christ, we are still sinners . . . Saved sinners to be sure, but sinners none-the-less. We keep on falling short of the expectations God has for us.

We men know painfully well that we aren't the kind of husbands and fathers and sons which Scripture says we should be. You women also know that when you compare your performance as wives and mothers and daughters with the demands of Scripture, you fall short as well. Children you know that you have not always obeyed and honored your parents the way God says you should. Not a one of us can say that we love the Lord our God with all our heart, mind, soul and strength. Gosh, we fall short there, don't we? And we fall equally short in loving our neighbor when we put stipulations on the kinds of neighbors we are willing to love. There is no question in our minds concerning that passage of Scripture. We know that we have sinned and fallen short of the Glory of God. But thanks be to God, he has not abandoned us in our sin. Because of the atoning death of Jesus Christ we can be forgiven and reconciled to God. If we simply acknowledge our sins with true repentance and confess them to the Lord, he will forgive us.

Christ is offering forgiveness of sins today. So we must examine ourselves and discover our sins. In 1 Corinthians 11:28 we read ". . . everyone should examine himself first, and then eat the bread and drink from the cup." Self examination is the necessary preparation for Holy Communion. With the Searchlight of Holy Scripture we must discover the specific sins in our lives. After confessing them at the Lord's altar, we must leave them there knowing that he has forgiven us. As we read in 1 John 1:8-9, "If we say we have no sin, we deceive ourselves, and the truth is not in us. If we confess our sins, he is faithful and just, and will forgive our sins and cleanse us from all unrighteousness." If we are truly sorry for our sins and desire to start over in life, God will relieve us of that burden of guilt with forgiveness and grant us new life. The sad thing is that too many of us don't really confess our sins. Too many of us just read through the confession at the beginning of worship without really examining our lives in light of the expectations of Scripture.

Some are like the little girl who went into a store one day to find a birthday present for her mother. She asked the salesgirl to show her some of the nicest cookie jars. At a counter where a large number of them were displayed, the youngster carefully lifted and replaced each lid. She looked rather disappointed as she came to the last one and said, "Maam, don't you have one with a lid that can be lifted and replaced without making any noise?" She was looking for a way to disobey without her mother knowing it! In the same way that youngster was looking for a way of not getting caught, or covering up her sin, so many Christians look for ways to sin more discreetly. But there is no way to sin and escape the all-seeing eye of God. The way to find relief from sin is not to try to fool God by hiding it, but to bring it out in the open! The way to get relief from sin is to come to the Lord's Table with humility and honestly confess your sins to God. Then you will be forgiven. Remember what he said about Holy Communion: "This cup is the new covenant in my blood, shed for you and for all people for the forgiveness of sin." Remembering that, you can then leave from the altar set free from your past sins ready to start anew! How do you spell relief for a troubled Soul? — J-E-S-U-S. Come to Jesus this morning and receive relief from your sin and guilt.

Second, Jesus can give relief from the burdens of life. There are so many people these days who are loaded down with the burdens and cares of this old world. Suicide rates have reached an all time high. People turn to drugs and alcohol in order to obliterate the pains they feel. Students turn to Transcendental Meditation and false religions in order to seek help to carry their burdens. Perhaps there are tensions between you and your spouse or you and your parents today. Maybe your job is bringing you more frustrations than fulfillment. Perhaps the threat of war and economic devastation are making the future bleak for you. Maybe your heart is breaking because of conflict in your relationship with your parents or your child. If there are burdens on your heart, then remember the invitation of Jesus in Matthew 11:28, "Come to me, all who labor and are heavy laden, and I will give you rest." Place those burdens in his hands. He is stronger and wiser than you. Trust him for guidance and help. Psalm 55:22 says "Cast your burden on the Lord, and he will sustain you." The Lord doesn't want you to worry. He doesn't want you to be weighed down with a burden of cares. He wants you to turn over all those problems to him and trust him to take care of you. In the same way that parents don't want their children to worry and fret about the necessities of life, God our Loving Parent doesn't want us to be burdened with worry. We are simply to cast our burdens upon the Lord, do the best we can with what he has given us and trust him to provide all we need! And he'll do it. God can be trusted! We need not worry for a moment. The really sad thing is that too many Christians don't trust the Lord enough to genuinely give their burdens over to him.

They are like the old lady who was walking along a dirt road one day. Strapped to the woman's back was a big pile of wood that she was carrying home. It was so heavy that she was bending over as she walked. Pretty soon a farmer and his family came along in a truck. He saw the old woman struggling along. He stopped his truck beside her and asked if she would like a ride. The lady smiled and said, "The sun is hot;

the load is heavy, Yes, it would be a big relief to ride on your truck." She climbed into the back of the truck and away they went. After they had gone several miles, the farmer looked into his mirror and noticed that the woman still had the heavy load of wood on her back. He stopped the truck, walked around to the back and said t her, "Maam, why don't you lay down that load. You no longer have to carry it! When I offered you a ride I was willing to carry both you and your burden."

The same is true in our Christian lives. When we responded to Christ's invitation to faith — to get on the Salvation Truck — he not only promised to carry us to Heaven, but he also promised to carry our burdens through life! Christ wants you to lay your burdens at his feet. He said, "Come to me all you that are weak and heavy ladened and I will give you rest." So when you come to the Lord's Table this morning I want you to place all your cares and troubles into the hands of the Lord and leave them there. Don't pick them back up again — leave them in his hands. He'll show you the way. He'll give you the strength. "Cast your burdens upon the Lord and he will sustain you!" How do you spell relief for a troubled heart? J-E-S-U-S! Jesus can give you relief from the burden of life!

The third and final thing I want to mention is this: Jesus can give relief from the fear of death. Psychologists say that the fear of death is the basic anxiety of human life. There are people who hate to go to sleep at night because they are afraid they will not wake up. Some folks won't get onto an airplane or even into an automobile for fear of losing their lives in an accident. There are people who live in constant fear of the dark, unknown curtain of death. But this should not be true for a Christian. We should not fear death for the very purpose of Christ's dying on the cross was to set us free from the power of death. Hebrews 2:14 tells us why Jesus came to this earth. That passage says "He did this so that through his death he might destroy the Devil, who has the power over death, and in this way set free those who were slaves . . . of their fear of death." We no longer have to be slaves of the fear of death. Christ has set us free from that basic anxiety. On the cross of Calvary as Jesus willingly poured out his life blood, Satan was defeated. He was conquered by the Victorious Resurrection of Jesus Christ. For us who believe, the fear of death has been overcome by the joy of eternal life.

As we gather around the Lord's Table today, let's remember Christ's sacrifice for us on the Cross of Calvary. As you eat the bread, think about his Body which was torn apart by the nails, the thorns and the spear. When you drink the wine think about his blood that was poured out as the ultimate sacrifice for our Salvation. Remember that he who was sinless and did not deserve death, willingly died so that we who deserve death might have eternal life. We need not fear death because we, who believe in Christ, have been promised eternal life. Jesus made a powerful promise about Holy Communion in John 6:54-55: "Whoever eats my flesh and drinks my blood has eternal life." If we come to the altar in faith, if we come to eat of the Living Bread from heaven, we receive the assurance of eternal life. Therefore we need not ever fear death because death has been conquered in the victorious Resurrection of Jesus Christ!

Perhaps you remember the story of the police officer who came upon a crying child in the park. When he asked why all the tears, she explained that she was lost. Determined to help her, the officer asked her some questions. The little girl did not know the name of her street or her house number. She didn't even know which direction her home was from there. The kind officer then asked her if there were any large buildings, lakes or landmarks near her home. At first she said no. But then she became excited and said, "Oh, I know, when I get to the cemetery, I'm almost there. My home is just beyond the Graveyard!"

Now that's true for us Christians too. Our eternal home is just beyond the Graveyard. That's why we need not fear death. When we breathe our last the Lord will be there to take us to our Heavenly Home. When you come to the altar today to eat the Bread and drink the Wine of Holy Communion, remember what Jesus said in John 6:54-55, "Whoever eats my flesh and drinks my blood, has eternal life." If you believe in Christ, the Bread of Life, you need not fear death for you have a Home in Heaven. If you trust Christ, if you believe his word, you'll see that Jesus spells relief from the fear of death.

How do you spell relief? Some folks spell it R-O-L-A-I-D-S. Well, Rolaids can help with stomach problems but only Jesus can help with Spiritual problems. In Holy Communion He gives us relief from sin and guilt, from the burdens of life, from the fear of death. How do I spell relief? J-E-S-U-S. He is our Lord and our Savior, and oh, what a relief that is!

6 | Communion Is
Reconciliation

2 Corinthians 5:17-18

Therefore, if anyone is in Christ, he is a new creation; the old has passed away, behold the new has come! All this is from God, who through Christ reconciled us to himself and gave us the ministry of reconciliation . . .

When Jackie and I have a serious disagreement about something related to our marriage or family, we will often go out to dinner to work things out. At a quiet table — with no children, TV, chores or distractions — we talk, share, think and unload. By mutual confession and compromise, we begin to remove the barrier between us and work toward restoring our relationship. By the time the meal has ended, reconciliation has occurred. The table becomes a place for reconciliation.

The Lord's Table is also a place for reconciliation. The LCA material *Welcome to the Lord's Table* which students use for Early Communion instruction, includes an exercise to demonstrate the dual nature of communion reconciliation. The teacher sets two dinner tables. On one of them are two places set on either side of the table — symbolizing that the Lord's Table is a place where God and you come into the personal and private fellowship. The other table is set with many plates and cups around it symbolizing that we are all in fellowship and communion with each other. The object lesson demonstrates for the pupils that during the Lord's Supper we are in communion with God and with each other. And in order to be in communion — close fellowship — with God and others, reconciliation is required. So, briefly today, I invite you to consider how the Lord's Table is a place for reconciliation.

First, communion is a time for being reconciled to God. This reconciliation begins with an acknowledgement that our sin has become a barrier in our relationship with God. God has not sinned against us. He has not forsaken a single promise to us. We have sinned against God. Communion is not at all like a husband and wife or two friends sitting down to work out a problem by mutual confession of fault because God is not guilty of forsaking his promises to us. There is no mutuality of guilt. It is only we who are guilty of jeopardizing the relationship. It is we who have sinned and not a single one of us is innocent. Romans 3:23 tells us, "All have sinned and fallen short of the glory of God." That "all" includes you and me. No matter how "good" we think we are, no matter what a "fine reputation" we have, no matter how "religious" we act, we all fall short of God's will for us as his people.

Let me illustrate: The story is told of two men who were trying to escape from an errupting volcano. As the molten lava gushed from the crater, they ran for their lives. All went well until they came to a broad stream of fiery lava which was about twenty feet across. Their only hope of safety was to leap over the river of molten mass. One of the men was old and arthritic; the other was a healthy young athlete. With a running start, they each tried to leap the stream. The first man jumped only a few feet before falling into the bubbling mass to his death. The younger man, with his great strength and athletic agility gave a mighty leap and jumped about eighteen of the twenty feet. Even though he jumped much farther than the first, the result was the same; he too died in the fiery lava. Both men fell short of the goal.

I don't know whether this story is true but it certainly illustrates a biblical truth: no matter how much effort we exert in trying to reconcile ourselves to God, we all fall short of the glory of God. We fall short as children — seldom obeying our parents as we should and giving them the honor which God commands. We fall short as husbands and wives — seldom fulfilling the vows we made on the day we were married. We fall short as parents when we do not act honorably toward our children and provide for them the kind of Christian example which we promised on the day of their baptisms. And it goes without saying, that we fall short as Christians when we adopt the thoughts, attitudes and ways of our hedonistic world.

God knows how miserably we fail to live up to his desires and expectations, but contrary to those men in the lava flow, he does not allow us to fall to eternal death. He invites us to come dine with him at his table of grace, where he will restore us to life by his forgiveness. We come to our Lord's Table in humility, being aware of our sins and knowing that he is aware of them too. We come with repentance, wanting God to strengthen us so we can turn away from our sin and overcome the temptations. We come with confession, knowing that God will remove the burden of our guilt and raise us up with new life. In Holy Communion, we come to dine with our Heavenly Father as prodigal children who have run away from home and squandered the good name he gave us. When we pour out our hearts to him at his table fully expecting to receive the scolding we deserve, we are surprised when God whispers to our hearts: "I love you my child — you are forgiven. Go with my strength and sin no more." As easily as that, God lovingly reconciles us to himself. In 2 Corinthians 5:19 the Apostle Paul wrote, "God was in Christ reconciling the world to himself." What God did in a cosmic sense through Christ's coming into the world, he does in an individual sense in Holy Communion. For in the Bread and Wine Christ will come to you and me to reconcile us to himself by forgiveness. So you see, the Lord's Table is a place for reconciliation with God.

The Lord's Table is also a beginning place of reconciliation with our neighbor. At the Lord's Table, Christ reminds us of our awesome responsibility: just as he has reconciled us to himself by forgiving us, we are to go and seek reconciliation with those who have sinned against us. We, following God's example, are to forgive those who have hurt, troubled, and wronged us! Just as God took the initiative to forgive us — we are to take the initiative to forgive others. God expects us to forgive them in our hearts and to let them know it by the way we show it in our lives. We are to begin treating them with love as though they had never done anything against us. Reconciliation with our neighbor is the direct result of our forgiveness. There can be no genuine reconciliation without genuine forgiveness.

There is a story which bears repeating today. It is about two African tribes who were bitter enemies. Warriors from each tribe dipped their spears into the other's blood, stole each other's wives, killed the other's children, and burned each other's villages. Then a Christian missionary proclaimed the Gospel to the rival chiefs and they were converted to Christ. In a few months, the warriors of each tribe were involved in daily Bible study. The Holy Spirit began to work in their lives and soon a miracle took place. The missionary had the privilege of seeing fruit come from faithful, loving witness for Christ. The people of these tribes demonstrated their unity in the Lord by kneeling at his table for Holy Communion. But then came the real display of forgiveness — after embracing members of the opposite tribe, they began to help each other rebuild their villages and replant their crops. You see, they realized that they had been reconciled to God by his forgiving love and they knew they had the responsibility to forgive and be reconciled to their neighbors . . . even their enemies.

Now the same is true for you and me today. When we rise from the Lord's Table this morning, we shall be completely forgiven and reconciled to God and he expects us to go and be reconciled to those who have sinned against us. That is God's will! We do not have the privilege of continuing to hold that grudge, hatred, or seething anger. We must forgive and be reconciled no matter how much we've been wronged; no matter how deeply we've been hurt, no matter how sorry we might be feeling for ourselves. Since God has fully forgiven us we have a responsibility to forgive others!

Today the Lord Jesus Christ is inviting you to join him at his table of reconciliation. We come with sin and guilt and humbly acknowledge that to him. In his gracious love he tells you that he forgives you and that you are reconciled to him. Then he strengthens you and instructs you to go share his forgiveness and be reconciled to those who have wronged you. The Lord's Table is a place for reconciliation! We are invited to come be reconciled to God and we are instructed to go be reconciled to others. Come, be forgiven by God. Go and do likewise.

7 | Communion Is **Response to an Invitation**

John 6:48-51

Jesus said, "I am the bread of life. Your fathers ate the manna in the wilderness, and they died. This is the bread which comes down from heaven, that a man may eat and not die. I am the living bread which came down from heaven; if any one eats of this bread, he will live forever; and the bread which I shall give for the life of the world is my flesh."

I want to begin this morning by reading an important letter to you (Note: Please amend this letter so it is appropriate for your congregation):

Dear Reverend (your name):

I extend to you personal greetings from the President of the United States!

As I am sure you are aware, our president has announced his candidacy for a second term in office. One of the important planks in his platform is to return our nation to her strong religious foundations, especially as they express themselves in voluntary prayer in public schools and the abortion issue.

To help build support for his position and to receive the opinions of the "grassroots religious people" of America, the President will sponsor a Religious Banquet and Forum at the White House on Sunday, June ____, 19____. Your congregation has been randomly selected to send two (2) representatives to the event as we gather 500 Lay Persons from all over this great nation of ours to share their concerns and convictions with the president. Please forward to us the names, addresses and phone numbers of your representatives by February 29th.

I thank you in the president's behalf as together we work toward strengthening America.

                         Kindest Regards,

                    White House Press Secretary

What do you think about that? Would you like to go to the White House and have dinner with the President? What if you already had something planned for that day, would you cancel it in order to go to Washington? If you were chosen as one of our representatives, how would you feel? Excited? Nervous? Joyful? Scared? Well, don't get overwhelmed by your feelings just yet because I do not really have a letter from the White House. That was a hoax. But even though I don't have a letter from the President inviting you to a banquet at the White House, I do have an invitation from the King of the Universe inviting you to a banquet at his table of grace. Jesus Christ, the Lord of Lords and King of Kings has invited you to a banquet in his honor today. Have you canceled other important plans in order to attend today? Do you value the Lord's invitation as highly as one from the President? How does his invitation make you feel? Excited? Nervous? Happy? Let me mention just two reactions we should have to Christ's invitation to dine with him at his table of grace.

First, we should be overwhelmed with joy! Just think

about it for a moment, won't you? Among all the millions of people in the world you and I have been invited to come dine at his table . . . that's exciting! We have been chosen to attend his great banquet and share with him all our burdens and pains . . . our sorrows and sins. The Lord wants you and me to dine with him . . . be in communion and intimate fellowship with the King of the Universe. That alone should fill us with joy. That is the reason for what Lutherans sing in the Post-Communion Canticle in their service. Just after all have received communion, they sing together: "Thank the Lord and sing his praise: Tell everyone what he has done. Let all who seek the Lord rejoice and proudly bear his name. He recalls his promises and leads his people forth in joy with shouts of thanksgiving. Alleluia! Alleluia!" (From the *Lutheran Book of Worship*) This is what we sing but is that what we show? Do we radiate with joy at the Lord's invitation to commune with him?

Too often, I fear, we come to communion with negative feelings and thoughts: We become impatient because the service will be longer rather than rejoicing in the added blessings we receive. We feel bored because we must sit and wait for everyone else to commune. We complain because there is no children's church or children's sermon. We approach the altar without having genuinely examined our lives in light of the Gospel. We kneel without having really confessed our sins and laid them on the Lord's table with repentant hearts. Therefore, we leave without experiencing the tremendous joy of knowing that we have been truly forgiven — our guilt removed — our relationship with God restored. For these and many other reasons, we oftentimes leave the banquet table looking sorrowful and sad rather than joyful and jubilant.

The German philosopher Nietzsche was very scornful of the Christians of his day. He said, "I would believe in their salvation if they looked a little more like people who have been saved." Too many of us do not look like saved people. Too many of us do not radiate with joy at being in communion with our Lord and King.

It reminds me of the little girl named Terri who was visiting her Uncle Joe on the farm. Her uncle was a very religious man . . . known by everyone to be a devoted Christian. But Uncle Joe never laughed or smiled and usually had a long, sad look on his face. Terri began to think that being a Christian meant being sad and serious all the time. That afternoon Terri went with Uncle Joe to the barn to feed the old mule. She noticed that the mule also had a long, sad face. When they put his food into the trough, the mule snorted and grunted very gruffly. Little Terri looked at her uncle and said, "That old mule is so sad and stern — I guess he's a Christian too."

It's sad when people get the impression that the Christian life is one of sadness and sorrow because nothing is farther from the truth. Joy is a hallmark of our lives in Christ. As the Apostle Paul wrote in Romans 15:13 "May the God of hope fill you with all joy and peace as you trust in him . . ." And again in 1 Thessalonians 5:16 he said, "Be joyful always." That joy should especially be evident in us today because the king of the universe has invited us to come to his banquet and dine at his table of grace! I hope that invitation makes you feel as joyful as it does me!

The second thing the Lord's invitation should make us feel is awe. Awe at being in his powerful presence! If indeed we were invited to a dinner at the White House one day, we would not make our acceptance of the invitation contingent upon what was to be served during the meal. It would not depend on the quality of the entertainment or how beautifully the banquet hall would be decorated. We would quickly accept the invitation just to be in the presence of the President. Being with the President would create a feeling of awe in most of our hearts. Well, how much greater awe would be generated in our hearts by being in the presence of the King of the Universe, Jesus Christ. We come into his powerful presence in a very unique and mysterious way when we partake of Holy Communion. The basic focus of our Lutheran theology of the Lord's Supper is the "real presence of Christ" . . . that in some mysterious, unexplainable way Christ is actually present, in with and under the elements of Bread and Wine . . . that it is, in fact, his supper . . . he is the host. It is Christ who has invited us, Christ who is feeding us with his body and his blood, Christ who is offering us his love, grace and forgiveness. He is here this morning, to do all that for us and more. If we genuinely believe that, then why aren't we filled with awe at being in his presence? I believe it is because we become too distracted by unimportant things. Perhaps you remember the dialogue from this childhood poem: "Pussy cat, pussy cat, where have you been?" "I've been to London to visit the Queen!" "Pussy cat, pussy cat, what did you do there?" "I chased a mouse from under her chair!" After hearing that we want to say, "You foolish cat. You were in the presence of the Queen and you spent your time chasing a mouse? What a waste of time! What a waste of opportunity!"

But are we not just as guilty of letting mundane, unimportant thoughts and things distract our attention from the king in our midst? We come to the Lord's Table thinking about how we look in our new suits rather than asking the Lord to dress us in righteousness. We come with minds cluttered with judgments against other worshipers mumbling, "How dare those persons kneel at this altar after what they've done!" We come to the King's table hoping that so-and-so in the congregation is noticing us rather than our taking notice of the King!

Many of our hearts are not filled with awe at being in the presence of Christ either because we don't care that he's here or because we don't really believe he is here. But I want to assure you with all my conviction and all my might that Jesus Christ is present with us today in our celebration of Holy Communion. When you come to the altar and receive these simple earthly elements of Bread and Wine, the King himself will dine with you. He's here this morning to hear your confession of sin. He's here to listen to you unburden your soul.

He's here to give you strength to overcome that enslaving habit. He's here to offer you his grace, his forgiveness, his love.

I may not be able to extend to you an invitation from our nation's President, but I can extend an invitation from our heavenly King. The Lord God himself wants you to come dine with him! So be filled with joy that the King of the Universe has invited you to his banquet of grace. And be filled with awe because the King himself will be present! Come, let us dine with the King!

8 | Communion Is **Repentance**

1 Corinthians 11:27-28

Whoever, therefore eats the bread or drinks the cup of the Lord in an unworthy manner will be guilty of profaning the body and blood of the Lord. Let a man examine himself, and so eat of the bread and drink of the cup.

A young soldier, who had just been promoted to the rank of sergeant, wanted to impress a private who came into his new office. The private saluted the officer and was about to speak when the sergeant said, "Just a minute soldier. I have to return an important phone call to the General." He picked up the telephone, dialed a number and said, "Hello General Johnson, I'm returning your call . . . oh, you need my advice? You'd like for me to meet with you and three other generals? . . . At 2:00 today? . . . Yes, I'll try to be there." Putting down the phone and with a smug look on his face, he turned to the private and said, "Now, soldier, what can I do for you?" The new recruit replied with a smile, "Nothing sir, I came to do something for you . . . I came to hook-up your telephone."

Needless to say the sergeant did not talk to the General nor did he make a good impression on the soldier. I'm sure that all his pretense was stripped away in that moment of eternal embarrassment. When you and I come to the Lord's Table for Holy Communion, we can come with pretense — pretending to be someone we are not — or we can come with sincere and humble repentance — acknowledging ourselves to be the sinners we are.

Christ invites us to come not pretensiously but penitently. In 1 Corinthians 11:27-28, the Apostle Paul gave the following instructions about Holy Communion: "Whoever therefore eats the bread or drinks the cup of the Lord in an unworthy manner will be guilty of profaning the body and blood of the Lord. Let a man examine himself, and so eat of the bread and drink of the cup." The Scripture calls us to honestly examine ourselves — not by comparing ourselves to other worshipers — not according to the standards of our society — but in the light of God's expectations of us as his children. We are to prepare for communion by calling to mind our dishonest deeds, our dishonorable thoughts and feelings, our less-than-gracious words, and lay them before the Lord with an attitude of repentance.

All of us would do well to remember that repentance is more than simply stating with our lips that "We're sorry, Lord." Repentance means showing with our lives that we are sorry. The word "repentance" is derived from a Latin word which means to "turn again" or "turn around." It implies a spiritual U-turn in life. A turning away from sinfulness and turning toward righteousness in the full knowledge that God promises to forgive the past and strengthen us for a new future.

A good example of this can be seen in John 8:1f. A woman had been caught in the very act of adultery — all her pretense was stripped away, to be sure. She was caught in her sin and was about to be stoned to death by the Jewish leaders. Jesus spoke to those who were about to execute her and said, "Let the one among you who has never sinned cast the first stone." When all of them left, Jesus said lovingly to the woman, "Neither do I condemn you. Go and sin no more." That's what repentance means — going away from a sin and with God's strength, not returning to it.

When we go to the Lord's Table, we should go as repentant sinners. Realizing that God has caught us in our sins. He knows how we act behind closed doors. He knows how we speak to our spouses. He knows how we dishonor our parents. He knows how we treat our children. He knows how we act on the job and at school. He even knows the secret thoughts and desires of our hearts. Realizing that God caught us in our sins should strip away our pretentious attitudes and leave us with penitent hearts. We go to the altar as sinners in need of forgiveness. We go to the Lord's Table as beggars who have nothing to offer but contrite, repentant, humble hearts . . . and indeed, that's all he wants from us.

It is most appropriate therefore, that we demonstrate the position of our hearts by the posture of our bodies. When we enter the presence of the King of Kings, those who are able should fall to bended knees in humble praise and adoration.

When Jackie and I had the privilege of touring Israel a few years ago, we were quite impressed by the Church of the Nativity in Bethlehem. One of the unique features of that massive sanctuary is the very small entrance way. The main door into the church is only about three feet high. It is almost necessary to crawl in. Our guide explained, "Like the wisemen of old, when we approach the birthplace of Christ, our Lord, we do so on bended knee."

It is quite fitting and proper that we kneel in the presence of our God. But the posture of the body should only be indicative of the position of the heart. Don't come to the Lord's Altar with pretense — pretending that you have no sin to turn away from, because you do. Don't come pretending that you are worthy of this sacrament, because you're not. Don't let your attitude be of a pretentious nature, but of a repentant nature. When you come to the altar, be aware of your sinfulness, be aware that you have not lived up to God's expectations of you as a Christian, be aware of your need for his gracious, loving forgiveness. When you eat the bread, remember his body hanging on that cross of agony, tearing, bleeding, writhing in pain. When you drink the wine, think about his blood oozing down his brow from the crown of thorns and pouring from his spear-punctured side. Focusing our hearts and minds on the fact that it was our sin — not his — that put Jesus on the cross, remembering that he endured that agonizing death to forgive you and me, should strip away all our pretense and bring us to our knees in genuine repentance.

The story is told of a young boy who was the only son of very faithful Christian parents. From the days of his early childhood, he was taken to Sunday School and worship. Both at Church and at home he was taught right from wrong. But when he became a teenager he fell in with the wrong crowd of friends. He began to tell lies and use profanity. He and his friends stole a car and became deeply involved with drugs. One evening his broken-hearted father sat down with him and tried to reason with him about how he was ruining his life. He said, "Son, don't you care that the language you use and the life you live do not at all reflect your Christian up-bringing?" The boy brashly replied, "No, Dad, I don't care!" The wise father then drove his son to the church where his parents had faithfully taken him as a child. He led the boy to the altar where there was a cross with a figure of Jesus hanging on it. He asked his son to kneel with him at the foot of that cross. The father pointed up at the figure of Jesus and said, "Son, tell him you don't care!" The boy looked up at the cross and said, "Jesus, I don't . . ." The words seemed to stick in his throat. Again he started, "Jesus, I really don't . . ." and again he stopped. Breaking into tears he said, "Jesus I'm sorry for what I've become. Please forgive me and help me become who you want me to be."

As that young man examined his sinful life in light of the love Christ had for him, the sacrifice Christ made for him, all of his pretenses were stripped away. He saw himself as he knew God saw him and that led him to repentance and change. When you come to the Altar this morning and kneel in the presence of the Lord, let the posture of your body reflect the position of your heart. Come, not in pretense, but in penitence.

The Lord already knows the sins of your life, your

tongue, your mind, and your heart. He has caught you in every sin you've committed, and surprise of surprises . . . he still loves you with all his broken heart. So come, God wants to forgive you. Come, God wants to strengthen you to change. Come into the special presence of Jesus Christ. Come, not in haughty pretense, but in humble penitence.

9 | Communion Is **Remedial**

Matthew 9:1-12

And getting into a boat he crossed over and came to his own city. And behold, they brought to him a paralytic, lying on his bed; and when Jesus saw their faith he said to the paralytic, "Take heart, my son; your sins are forgiven." And behold, some of the scribes said to themselves, "This man is blaspheming." But Jesus, knowing their thoughts, said, "Why do you think evil in your hearts? For which is easier to say, 'Your sins are forgiven,' or to say, 'Rise and walk?' But that you may know that the Son of man has authority on earth to forgive sins" — he then said to the paralytic — "Rise, take up your bed and go home." And he rose and went home. When the crowds saw it, they were afraid, and they glorified God, who had given such authority to men. As Jesus passed on from there, he saw a man called Matthew sitting at the tax office; and he said to him, "Follow me." And he rose and followed him. And as he sat at table in the house, behold, many tax collectors and sinners came and sat down with Jesus and his disciples. And when the Pharisees saw this, they said to his disciples, "Why does your teacher eat with tax collectors and sinners?" But when he heard it, he said, "Those who are well have no need of a physician, but those who are sick."

One day three doctors were in a conversation about what they considered to be the biggest contributing factor for most people's poor health. The first one said he was convinced that the key to most people's poor health was how much food they eat. The second physician said she did not agree. In her opinion the biggest factor is not how much they eat but what they eat. Finally the third doctor injected his thoughts on the matter saying, "As important as diet is, the biggest factor in people's poor health is not how much they eat or what they eat. The biggest factor is what's eating them." And you know he's right. That is not only true for our physical health but it is also true for our spiritual health. The Great Physician, Jesus Christ, says that what's really eating us — the thing which has permeated our lives and affects all we do — is sin.

In Holy Communion, Christ, the Great Physician, comes to us offering a remedy for our sin that is eating us. In the bread and wine, he comes to heal our hearts with his gracious love. He comes to strengthen us in our weakness and release us from all that holds us in bondage. He comes to forgive our sinfulness! Therefore, whenever Holy Communion is offered at this altar we should be here. We should come regularly because our need is great. We should come eagerly because we are sick with sin and in him is healing!

Martin Luther wrote in 1529, ". . . anyone who does not desire to receive the Lord's Supper at least three or four times during the year, despises the Sacrament and is no Christian." (Ewald Plass; *What Luther Says*, Vol. II, p. 814-815) Luther was never one to mince words. He was quite emphatic about the importance of Christians receiving the Lord's Supper on a regular basis. Let's examine why we should come to the Lord's Table eagerly and regularly.

First, we come because we need to come. If you were sick with a disease which you thought was incurable and you heard of a certain doctor who was able to give you a remedy for your illness, there is very little, if anything that would prevent your going to that doctor. Well, the disease which plagues all humanity is sin. Left alone, untreated, it is terminal. "The wages of sin is death!" says Romans 6:23. But there is one, and only one, physician who has the remedy which will set us free from our sickness of sin and that is the Great Physician — Jesus Christ. He is the only giver of forgiveness. He is our only source of salvation. He is our only hope for healing. So we must not permit anything to prevent us from meeting the Great Physician at his table of grace.

When I was the pastor of Trinity Church in Georgetown, South Carolina, I noticed a curious thing. There was a lady who never came to the altar for communion. Oh, she was in worship every Sunday and was in the congregation when we celebrated the sacrament. She simply chose not to come to the altar. After several months, I asked her about it and she told me that she had been divorced several years before, and since that time she had not considered herself worthy to receive communion. In essence what she was saying was that she knew herself to be a sinner and because of that she felt unworthy. I helped her understand that all of us are sinners — Romans 3:23 says, "All have sinned and fallen short of the glory of God" — therefore not one of us is worthy to partake of the Lord's presence in Holy Communion. But the recognition of our unworthiness — the knowledge of our sin — our self-confessed need of forgiveness is the very reason we should come. Since we know we are sick we need to come to the source of help and healing.

I once read the following definition of the Church: "The Church is not a museum for saints; it is a hospital for sinners!" I like that definition. We are a family of people sick with sin who come to the Great Physician for healing and strength. We are a house of unworthy servants who come to our gracious master for help. Never let anything prevent your coming to Holy Communion — especially not your feeling of unworthiness — because implicit in that feeling is an acknowlegement of your sin . . . a recognition of your disease. And the proper diagnosis of a disease is the first step toward healing.

Yes, sin is what's eating all of us, and only Jesus Christ, the Great Physician, has the remedy for it. So the first reason we should come to Holy Communion is because we need to come!

Not only do we come because of our need but we also come in obedience to the command of Christ. The Great Physician has given us a prescription to provide the remedy for our sin. In 1 Corinthians 11:24, Paul wrote what Jesus said about Holy Communion, "Do this in remembrance of me!"

In the same way a doctor, who really cares about a patient, will prescribe a certain kind of medication or activity, Jesus has ordered us to come to him in Holy Communion and to do so regularly and faithfully. In Matthew 11:28 the Lord said, "Come to me all you who labor and are heavy laden and I will give you rest . . . for your weary soul." God loves us. He does not like to see us eaten-up with guilt and burdened with cares and worries so he commands that we come to him. When we unburden our hearts to him in prayer, he gives us comfort. When we confess our sins to him, he grants us assurance of forgiveness. When we place our problems into his loving hands, he gives us rest from those struggles. Like a loving parent having to remind a child to take medicine because it's good for him, Jesus commands that we come to Holy Communion because through the bread and wine the Great Physician comes to us as the remedy for our sin. Therefore we come to communion in obedience to Christ our King.

When Leonard Woods, president of Bowdoin College, was in France, he was invited to dine with the King. When he arrived at the palace that evening, he was met by the great ruler who said courteously, "We did not know we were to have the pleasure of your company tonight. You did not answer the invitation." Dr. Woods replied, "Your Majesty, I thought the invitation of a king was to be obeyed, not answered." This morning, you and I have an invitation from the King of this universe. Jesus Christ, the Great Physician, is inviting you to bring to him what's eating you . . . all your hurts . . . all your struggles . . . all your doubts . . . all your sins, and he will give you help, hope and healing. So we come to communion in our unworthiness first because we need to and second, in obedience to his command.

If sin is eating you — and it is — come to the Great Physician for his remedy. Come in unworthiness . . . come in obedience . . . come expecting a miracle of healing in your soul.

Worldwide Communion Sunday

10 | Communion Is **Reunion**

1 Corinthians 10:16-17

The cup of blessing which we bless, is it not a participation in the blood of Christ? The bread which we break, is it not a participation in the body of Christ? Because there is one bread, we who are many are one body, for all partake of the one bread.

When I think about the world we live in, the one descriptive word that leaps forth in my mind is "division". Nations are divided against other nations. It's East versus West. Jews versus Arabs. Communism versus Capitalism. The Haves versus the Have-nots. There are so many divisions in our world. Our own nation is split into hundreds of shattered fragments as well. Just a quick glance at the newspaper reveals the rift that greed has brought between labor and management. There is anger and distrust between Blacks and Whites. And the Rich keep themselves separate from the Poor. There is so much division in this "One nation under God — indivisible — with liberty and justice for all." But I suppose it is not too shocking to see all the division in our world and nation. We've come to expect it as a part of life. But it is very shocking when we think about all the division, separation and strife that exist in the world-wide Christian Church. And the Church is divided, you know. There are Protestants who refuse to commune at the same altar with Catholics, and Catholics who refuse to commune with Protestants. The Church is divided by the fundamentalists who will have nothing to do with the liberals. There are charismatics who think they are spiritually superior to other Christians who do not speak in tongues. And there are some denominations which actually believe that if you don't belong to their church, you will not go to heaven.

Perhaps you've heard the story about the man named Sam who died and went to heaven. St. Peter met him in order to give him a guided tour of the heavenly mansion. As they were walking down one of the main corridors Sam heard gothic chants coming from within one of the rooms. St. Peter explained that behind that door were all of the Catholics, Lutherans and Episcopalians — because they like liturgical worship.

As they came to another door, Sam heard lots of hand clapping and foot-stomping. St. Peter explained that in the room were the Churches of God, the Pentecostal Holiness and the charismatics because they like high emotion in their worship.

When they reached the end of the corridor they came to a room which was set off by itself. From that door, not a sound came. Sam was just fixing to ask who was in there when St. Peter put his finger to his lips and told him not to make a sound because in that room were the Baptists and we like to let them go on thinking that they are the only ones here.

Now of course Baptists no longer officially teach that doctrine, but there are Christian groups which still think they have a corner on salvation — that if you are not a member of their church you will have no place in heaven. And because of such closed minded beliefs, because of such spiritual snobbery, those Christians will have little to do with the likes of you and me. They will not even share Holy Communion with us at the Lord's Table. Now that's sad when the Lord's Supper becomes a symbol of division.

This is not only true between differing denominations but it is even true within denominations. The Missouri Synod Lutheran Church will not allow other Lutherans to partake of the Lord's Supper in one of their worship services because they are not a member of that denomination (the same is true for the Wisconsin Synod). They can worship together, study the Bible together, and even send their pastors to the same seminaries, but they will not allow others to share Holy Communion with them. Doctrines of communion have become a point of division even within denominations of Christians. In my opinion it is a shame when Christians of all denominations cannot be united in Holy Communion.

The Lord's Table should not be a place of division but a place of solidarity . . . a place of oneness for all of God's people. That is exactly what God intended for communion. We see in John 17:21 that just after Jesus instituted the Lord's Supper, he prayed to the Father that his disciples "may all be one." We should not be divided — we should be one and as Ephesians 4:3-5 says, we should do our "best to preserve the unity which the Spirit gives . . .(for) there is one Lord, one faith, one baptism; there is one God and Father of all." All who trust Jesus, as Lord of their lives, are one with us — no matter what denomination they belong to. And the Lord's most precious symbol of that oneness is Holy Communion. St. Paul describes that for us in 1 Corinthians 10:17 when he writes, "In the same way that there is one loaf of bread, we who are many, are one body, for we all partake of the one loaf."

There should be special oneness felt among all Christians today on this Worldwide Communion Sunday. This is the closest that we can get to sharing Holy Communion with Christians of all denominations. This very day Christians all over the world will be receiving the Body and Blood of Jesus Christ with penitent hearts. Today we are all unified around the Lord's altar by a common loaf made, not from wheat or barley, but from the body of the Lord himself who said in John 6:35 "I am the Bread of Life. Anyone who comes to me will never be hungry." All who feast on the Bread of Life are united in Christ. No matter what denomination, no matter how rich or poor, no matter what race or national background, when we come to the Lord's Table all of our differences and disputes should dissolve, so that we might celebrate that which unites us — our one faith, one hope, one Lord — symbolized by one loaf.

But, too often even during this Holy Meal, Christians are divided because people prefer to emphasize their differences rather than our unity as one family in Jesus Christ.

One Sunday morning a lady confided in her pastor that she had invited her family and relatives to dinner the night before. She had sacrificed many long hours planning and preparing the meal in the hope that the family could enjoy their time together. But her hopes were smashed and her hard work was made futile as family tensions, petty jealousies and ridiculous bickering caused everyone to leave early. The young lady was in tears as she told her pastor, "It seems that the more we are together, the further we drift apart. Why can't we just enjoy the fact that we are a family and overlook our differences?" I suspect we are all saddened when our families are torn asunder by those who want to bicker, argue and constantly complain. Did you ever stop to wonder how it must sadden our Lord when he sees the same thing going on in his family — the Christian Church — when one group won't commune with another because of some minor point of doctrine? Jesus sacrificed more than long hours — he sacrificed his very life on the cross in order to prepare this feast of forgiveness for you and me. His body was broken so that we might be one. His blood was poured out so that we might be pulled together into one family of faith. Since he has sacrificed so much for us, for his sake, we must lay aside our differences, our arguments, our complaints and celebrate our oneness in him. The Lord's Table should be a place of solidarity where Christians from all backgrounds might celebrate our unity in Christ Jesus.

Maybe you and I can do little to encourage other denominations to let us commune with them. But on this Worldwide Communion Sunday we can celebrate the fact that we are moving in the right direction as Christians all over the world are partaking in one loaf called the Bread of Life — one loaf who is Jesus Christ himself. But we can do something to increase our unity in this congregation. When you come to the Lord's Table today, put all bickering, pettiness and anger from your heart. Forget all of those things which divide you from your brother and sister and focus on the common loaf which unites us as God's Family. That common loaf reminds us of Jesus Christ who is the Bread of Life. It is the Bread of Life who unites us!

11 | Communion Is **Reformed**

Luke 22:19-20

Then he took a piece of bread, gave thanks to God, broke it, and gave it to them, saying, "This is my body, which is given for you. Do this in memory of me." (TEV)

In the same way, after the supper he took the cup, saying, "This cup is the new covenant in my blood, which is poured out for you."

Martin Luther was reared by very strict Catholic parents. They rightly believed that the devil was real and constantly present. They believed that God was to be feared and respected. So anytime young Martin or any of their other children did something "devilish," they were severely punished.

Luther told about the day that he stole a hazelnut. When his mother found out about what he had done, she whipped him with a cane until blood came from his skin. Cruel and unjust punishment? I should say. But Luther said his mother meant well. She was determined that he know right from wrong and that he learn to fear the righteousness of God. And fear God he did! His fear of the Lord plagued him throughout his early years of development and even continued when he became a priest. All of his fear of God came to a head when he celebrated his first Mass, his first service of Holy Communion.

Luther believed, as the Church taught, that a priest was closer to God than any other human, except the Pope of course.

Only a priest had the privilege of talking directly to God, everyone else had to pray through the priests. Only a priest had the privilege of performing the miracle of the Mass: transforming the Bread and Wine into the Body and Blood of Christ.

Despite these privileges, as his first celebration of Holy Communion approached, Luther became more and more frightened. He knew that he was not worthy to hold in his hands the flesh and blood of Christ. He wasn't sure that he was ready to talk directly to God. What if he did or said something wrong in Mass? What if he mishandled the Bread and Wine? God would surely be angry and punish him severely and swiftly as his parents had done years before.

Needless to say, when his first Mass began, Luther was quite nervous. When he came to the part in the service where he was to lift the bread and cup, saying, "We offer to thee, the living, the true and eternal God . . . ." his voice left him completely. He thought to himself, "With what tongue shall I address the Almighty God? For I am but dust and ashes, full of sin, and I am speaking to the living, eternal and true God." His fear made him speechless! Luther did manage to get his voice back and finish his first Mass. But that even exemplified his innermost feelings about Holy Communion. At that point in his life he accepted the Roman Catholic teaching of transubstantiation. The doctrine that the bread and wine actually changed into the body and blood of Christ when the priest spoke the proper words at the altar.

Communion was mysterious and awesome. The Church was so afraid that lay people might spill the wine and in that way profane the sacred blood of Christ. The cup, the chalice, was withheld from the worshipers. The people received only the bread of Holy Communion. It was the priest's responsibility to drink the wine in behalf of the Congregation. In the same way that it was his responsibility to offer the body and blood of Christ as a sacrifice to God for the sins of the people.

Well as I said, in his early years as a priest Luther believed in the doctrine of transubstantiation and in the practice of withholding the wine from the laity. But in the midst of the Reformation, he rejected both the doctrine and the practice. He wrote that transubstantiation "is a monstrous word for a monstrous idea. The bread remains bread and the wine remains wine." (Theodore Tappert, *The Lord's Supper*, p. 12) Since the bread and wine do not actually change into the body and blood of Jesus, Luther argued that there was no reason to withhold the chalice of wine from the congregation. Therefore one of the radical changes which the Reformation brought was the serving of both bread and wine in Holy Communion.

Luther not only rejected the Doctrine of Transubstantiation — that the Communion Elements changed into Christ's Body and Blood, he also rejected the memorial view. This theological position held that the bread and wine were merely symbols to remind us of our Lord's Body which was broken and his Blood which was spilled on the Cross of Calvary. To be sure, they do remind us of what Christ did for us through his atoning death he said, "Do this in remembrance of Me." But for Luther and Lutherans, Communion is more than a memorial service in which we remember what the Lord did for us in the past. Holy Communion is a celebration of what he is doing for us in the present and what he promises to do for us in the future.

Lutherans believe not in transubstantiation or the memorial view but in the real presence of Christ in Holy Communion. They believe that Christ himself comes to the recipient — not simply the metaphysical substances of his flesh and blood. When we gather for Holy Communion, we believe that Christ is our host. He is really present in, with and under the forms of Bread and Wine to invite us to meet him at his Table of Grace. As we eat the bread and drink the wine in repentant faith, Christ comes to give us "forgiveness of sins, life and salvation" as Luther wrote in his Small Catechism.

For Lutherans, Holy Communion is not a sacrifice to God which some human priest makes in our behalf. It is not our remembering what Christ did for us on the Cross. Communion is not anything a human being does. It is something that God does for us! He comes with forgiveness of sins. He brings assurance of salvation. He gives strength for battling temptation and living the abundant life. Psalm 55:22 says, "Cast your burdens upon the Lord and he will sustain you." Many of us become burdened with worries, concerns and problems. In Holy Communion, Christ invites us to come to him with repentant hearts, confessing our sins and he will relieve us of our burden of guilt with the assurance of forgiveness.

Christ is present in this special meal of grace. Christ is here to relieve us of our burdens if we'll let him. The trouble is that we won't trust our Lord enough to cast our burdens on him. Too many of us choose to hold on to our burdens as we add today's pain onto yesterday's sorrow and top it all off with worry about tomorrow. So many of us have not learned the tremendous lesson which Jesus taught in the Sermon on the Mount (Matthew 6:34) saying "Do not worry about tomorrow for tomorrow will have worries enough of its own." God wants us to trust him to be present with us and then just live one day at a time!

In her book *Nestle, Don't Wrestle,* Corrie ten Boom tells an old Dutch parable about the clock which had a nervous breakdown. The clock had just been finished and placed on the store shelf with two older clocks on either side. One was an old table top clock which was very negative about life. To the new young clock, he said, "So, you're just starting out in life . . . I feel sorry for you. Just think for a bit and see how many ticks lay ahead of you. You'll never make it! You'd better stop now." The new clock took the advice and began counting the ticks: "Each second requires two ticks which means 120 per minute, 172,800 per day; 1,209,600 ticks per week for fifty-two weeks — and that makes a total of 62,899,200 ticks in a year! Horrors!" said the new clock and then he had a nervous breakdown and stopped ticking. On the other side was a wise old mantel clock who overheard the conversation. She chimed in and said, "You silly youngster, don't listen to all his negativism. He's been unhappy for years and wants you to share his misery. Think about it another way: How many ticks do you have to tick at one time?" The new clock replied, "Only one, I suppose." "That's right!" said the mantel clock, "That's not so hard is it — just one tick at a time. And one more thing . . . don't ever think about the next tick until you have finished your last tick." Soon the new clock was running smoothly — just one tick at a time.

Let's make a pledge today that we are going to trust God and live one day at a time. Let's not permit our pain, burden of sin and our worries to mount up, instead let's cast all that into the hands of him who loves us — Jesus Christ our Lord. He cannot give us rest and renew our strength if we are unwilling to lay down our burdens of sin, pain, and worry.

Jesus is really present, in a special and mysterious way this morning in our celebration of Holy Communion. He is not here to change the bread and wine into his body and blood. He is not here simply to help us remember his great sacrifice for us on the Cross of Calvary. Jesus is here to forgive us, to strengthen us, to save us, to love us. He is here inviting us: "Come to me, my heavy laden children and I will give you rest. Cast your burdens upon me and I will sustain you!"

When you come to the Altar today I want you to believe, as Luther did, that Christ is really present in our celebration of his Holy Supper. Confess your sins to our Lord and hear him say that you are forgiven. Place all your cares, fears, worries and burdens into Christ's loving hands and know that he will strengthen and sustain you. Then leave the Altar refreshed, renewed and rejoicing.

12 | Communion Is **Rejoicing In Christ's Return**

1 Thessalonians 3:9-13

For what thanksgiving can we render to God for you, for all the joy which we feel for your sake before our God, praying earnestly night and day that we may see you face to face and supply what is lacking in your faith? Now may our God and Father himself, and our Lord Jesus, direct our way to you; and may the Lord make you increase and abound in love to one another and to all men, as we do to you, so that he may establish your hearts unblamable in holiness before our God and Father, at the coming of our Lord Jesus with all his saints.

In my file for this First Sunday in Advent, I found an article from "The State" newspaper dated July 27, 1980. The article, entitled "Saga of a Heavenly Hitchhiker," said the Arkansas State police had received two reports — both on a particular Sunday — that a clean-cut, well-dressed hitchhiker had disappeared from cars traveling along highways in the state. The stories went like this: "A middle-aged couple was driving along US 65 between Pine Bluff and Little Rock. They were not folks prone to pick up hitchhikers, but saw this good-looking, nicely dressed man walking along the highway. Assuming he needed transportation, they offered him a lift. He said, 'Yes, thank you, I'll ride with you for a ways.' While they drove, the conversation turned to world affairs and then the mysterious man said, 'Jesus is coming' — either twice or three times — and then vanished from the moving vehicle." I do not know if this incident is true or a fanatical hoax, but I do believe its message is true — Jesus is coming again. I believe it because that is his promise.

The return of Christ is one of the central themes of the Advent Season which is beginning today. The word "Advent" is derived from two Latin words, "Ad" and "Veneo" — meaning "To Come." The season directs our thoughts to the past and to the future: Looking to the past we remember Christ's first coming to this world as the babe of Bethlehem to redeem Humanity from the bondage to sin, death and the Devil. That coming of the Messiah was promised in Scripture and those prophecies have been completely fulfilled. Looking toward the future we think about the New Testament promises that Christ will return to this earth with glory and power as King of Kings to complete our redemption.

In Acts 1:11, just after Jesus had ascended into heaven, two angels told his disciples, "This same Jesus, who has been taken from you into heaven will come back in the same way you have seen him go." In the Second Lesson for today, the Apostle Paul made reference to ". . . the coming of our Lord Jesus with all his saints," which he wrote about in detail in the fourth chapter of 1 Thessalonians. In today's Gospel from Luke 21, our Lord himself promised that he will return and he told us about the signs which will precede his return. Jesus said, "There will be signs in sun and moon and stars, and upon the earth . . . for the powers of the heavens will be shaken. And then they will see the Son of man coming in a cloud with power and great glory." That text is saying the entire universe will resonate with Christ's victorious return.

Christ gave us his promise that he will come again and has provided us with signs to help us anticipate his return. The unfortunate thing is, throughout history people have studied those signs and attempted to predict the exact time of

Christ's return. In the early nineteenth century, William Miller, a New England farmer of Baptist background, began to study the Scriptures of Daniel and Revelation. As a result of his study, he concluded that the second coming of Christ would occur on March 21, 1843. In 1831, William Miller began to warn the people of America about this cataclysmic event. It is estimated that about 100,000 people were converted to Miller's interpretation of the Scriptures. At the beginning of 1843, Miller proclaimed: "This year ... o glorious year, the trumpet of jubilee will be blown ... This year, the looked-for year of years, has come!"

March 21, 1843, came and went but there was no blowing of the archangel's trumpet — Christ did not return. Miller came to the conclusion that he had made the mistake of using a Roman calendar instead of a Jewish calendar. After recalculating, he announced that the second coming of Christ would be in October, 1844. But again the day came and there was no sounding trumpet, no Christ in the clouds, no second coming of the Lord.

In every generation there are those well-meaning Christians who use the Bible as a kind of crystal ball with which they try to predict the future return of Christ. But the Lord told us plainly that such efforts are futile! In Matthew 24:36 Jesus said the following about the time of his return: "But of that day and hour no one knows, not even the angels of heaven, nor the Son, but the Father only." You see, it is impossible for us to know when Christ will return. He has chosen not to reveal that information to us. He wants us to live by faith, not sight or guesswork. He simply wants us to take him at his word, trusting him to return when he determines the time to be right. Not knowing when he will come gives us the privilege and responsibility of living in constant preparedness for the coming of our Lord. We are to live each day as if we expect Christ to return in the very next moment.

Even though we cannot predict Christ's second coming,

we can expect it without doubt! Our Lord will do what he has promised to do! Think about it: God promised to send the Messiah into the world and that promise was fulfilled when Jesus was born in Bethlehem — an event we are now preparing to celebrate. God also promised that Jesus will return as victorious Lord of Lords and King of Kings. We can expect him to come when he determines the time to be right. And when Christ comes, our redemption — which he won for us on the cross of Calvary — will be given to us completely as he rescues us from the pains and perils of this life. As the Gospel for today says, "On that day we are to look up and raise our heads, because our redemption will be drawing near." What a glorious day that will be!

But between now and then, which may be two minutes, two years, or 2000 years, you and I and all believers must wait — hopefully and patiently. Waiting patiently is almost a lost virtue in these days of instant foods, microwave cooking, and computer speed answers. Patience is specially hard when we are waiting for something we anticipate with great joy and excitement such as the glorious return of Christ. Think of how hard it is to wait for that new family car you ordered or the new bike you've been promised. Think of how difficult it is for students at this time of year to wait patiently for the Christmas Vacation. Notice during the next few weeks how hard it is for children to see all the signs of the season and still wait patiently for Christmas Morning.

The same struggle is experienced by us Christians who try to wait patiently for the return of Christ our Lord. We eagerly anticipate the day when our complete redemption will be given to us. It is hard to be patient as we wait for the day when we will be set free from all the pain and temptation we experience in this earthly life. It's hard to wait patiently for the day when we will be united with Christ and reunited with those we love who have died before us. It's difficult to be patient as we wait for that glorious heavenly banquet in which we will feast with God and his people and he will wipe away all tears from our eyes.

On this Sunday after Thanksgiving, how well I remember the Thanksgiving Days of my youth. What a special time that was for our family. How we enjoyed the meal and just being together. I can remember how hard it was to wait for the delicious meal Mother would cook all the morning. The house was permeated with mouth-watering aromas. At times my patience would wear thin — I'd go into the kitchen and ask Mother how much longer it would be until we ate. Inevitably she would say, "Be patient son. We'll eat when all is ready." To help me wait, she would pinch off a little piece of turkey or bread as a foretaste of the delicious banquet that was soon to be enjoyed by our whole family.

That illustrates for me how it is in God's family as we wait for the heavenly banquet. In a similar way, we ask, "How long, O Lord? How much longer do we have to wait for your return. How long do we have to endure the pains, burdens, sorrows and temptations of this life? How much longer will it be before we can celebrate the heavenly banquet with you and all your family?" Then the Lord whispers to us, "Be patient my child, be patient. It will be a while longer for all is not yet ready." Then Christ comes to us in Holy Communion and gives us a foretaste — just a sampling — of the glorious banquet he is preparing for us in the halls of heaven.

The menu of bread and wine is not the important thing for those are only the earthly channels through which we receive heavenly blessings. No, we get something better than food. In Holy Communion, God gives us a foretaste of the fellowship with him which will be made perfect on that day of redemption when we will see him face to face. He gives us a nibble of his graciousness as he forgives our sins and strengthens us to go on and face tomorrow with him. God gives us a sampling of his love as he invites us to lay all of our burdens into his hands and leave them there as we anticipate the day when he will make sure we have no burdens at all to bear.

But in Holy Communion, we must remember, we receive only a morsel, only a sampling, only a foretaste of what Christ has in store for us around his heavenly banquet table where we will feast with him for eternity. The Bread and Wine of which we are about to partake serve only as an appetizer to help us wait more patiently, more expectantly and more faithfully for Christ's visible and victorious return to this earth.

So on this first Sunday in Advent, we realize that we don't need a heavenly hitchhiker to tell us the news, for we have the promise of the King himself that Jesus is coming again! We cannot predict the exact time of Christ's return but we can expect his return at any time. As we wait patiently to see our Lord face to face, let's gather at his Table and receive a foretaste of what's in store for us.

First Communion Day for [Six] Children

13 | Communion Is **Running No More**

Mark 9:38-50

John said to him, "Teacher, we saw a man casting out demons in your name, and we forbade him, because he was not following us." But Jesus said, "Do not forbid him, for no one who does a mighty work in my name will be able soon after to speak evil of me. For he that is not against us is for us. For truly, I say to you, whoever gives you a cup of water to drink because you bear the name of Christ, will by no means lose his reward. Whoever causes one of these little ones who believe in me to sin, it would be better for him if a great millstone were hung round his neck and he were thrown into the sea. And if your hand causes you to sin, cut it off; it is better for you to enter life maimed than with two hands to go to hell, to the unquenchable fire. And if your foot causes you to sin, cut it off; it is better for you to enter life lame than with two feet to be thrown into hell. And if your eye causes you to sin, pluck it out; it is better for you to enter the kingdom of God with one eye than with two eyes to be thrown into hell, where their worm does not die, and the fire is not quenched. For every one will be salted with fire. Salt is good; but if the salt has lost its saltness, how will you season it? Have salt in yourselves, and be at peace with one another.

Bob Roberts tells a story which appeared in the newspaper

some time back about a mother of eight children in Darlington, Maryland. She had been visiting the neighbor next door and when she returned home, she found her five youngest children huddled in the center of the living room on her new carpet. The children were playing excitedly with some thing very wiggly and furry. Upon closer examination, she discovered to her dismay that the children were gathered around a family of skunks! In horror of what could happen she screamed, "Run children, run to your rooms." Hearing that each child grabbed a skunk and ran to their bedrooms. I'm sure that's not at all what the mother had in mind. I can imagine that those children carried the smell of skunk with them for several weeks thereafter.

That could very well be a parable of human life. No matter how hard we try, no matter how far we run, we cannot run away from the stench of sin in our lives. For like those children, we carry with us that basic nature which is rebellious to God wherever we go and whatever we do.

Psalm 51:5 says: "Behold, I was brought forth in iniquity, and in sin did my mother conceive me." Each of us was born with the propensity to sin. And that propensity, that tendency to rebel against God, manifests itself in many ways in our daily lives. It permeates our thought patterns, our actions, and our relationships. It is a powerful force in our lives! It leads us into believing that the world should revolve around our every whim and desire. It permits us to live a philosophy which says, "If it feels good, do it." It tells us "If it's OK for everyone else to do it, it's OK for you to do it too!" It convinces us, "Hey, you're the Captain of your soul — the King of your own Life — have it your way!"

We need no convincing about the presence of our sinful nature. We know how it can wreck relationships. We've experienced the pain it can cause as we seek momentary pleasure without consideration for the long-range results. We know that the Apostle Paul was correct when he wrote in Romans 3:23: "All have sinned and fall short of the glory of God."

But on this Sunday when [six] of our young people are receiving Holy Communion for the very first time, we are reminded that something can be done about our sin.

In today's Gospel, we learn that there is something we can do. We can know our weaknesses and exercise caution about the circumstances and situations which will lead us into sinful action. In the text from Mark 9, Jesus said, "If your hand or foot causes you to sin, cut it off . . . If your eye causes you to sin, pluck it out . . ." The Lord points out to us that sinful actions are a serious matter and serious steps should be taken to insure that those actions are not repeated because of the harm they cause us and others.

Let me give you a few examples: Do you have a hot temper which strikes at others as fierce and quick as a bolt of lightning? Then perhaps Jesus' word to you is to remove yourself from those situations which call forth your anger just long enough for you to be able to talk calmly and sensibly about the problem and find a solution. Perhaps you find that lust can rise quickly in your heart and mind? Than the Lord would tell you to be careful about the movies you see and magazines you look at. Maybe you have difficulty saying "No" to your friends when they want you to participate with them in activities which you know are wrong. Christ would tell you to chop-off those relationships and find other friends. Perhaps you drink too much alcohol or smoke too much? Jesus would say to change your daily routines and seek help to be set free from enslaving habits which do nothing but harm your body and relationships.

On and on the list could go but you can make your own which is appropriate to your life. The point Jesus makes is that sinful activity should be dealt with in a serious and severe manner. We are to cut ourselves off from the activity before it cuts us off from God. We should do everything within our power to avoid those persons, places, situations, and activities which we permit to lead us into sinful acts. We are to be cautious and careful.

I am reminded of a very wealthy man who was interviewing three persons in order to hire a chauffeur. When talking with each, he pointed to a narrow road near his home which ran very close to a steep cliff and asked them, "Suppose you were driving on that road and came to the cliff, how close to the edge could you safely drive?" One man said, "I could easily drive within a foot of the edge without blinking an eye." The second one said, "Sir, I could get within six inches of the edge without your having to worry a bit." The third applicant remained silent. When pressed for an answer, she replied, "Sir, I would never risk your life or mine. I would seek another route." The lady, the cautious one, was hired. In essence, this is the same kind of caution Jesus tells us to exercise regarding the persons, places and situations which we know will lead us into sinful action. We are to stay away from them — find another route! That's the first thing that you and I can do about our sinful activities.

The second thing we are reminded of on this first Communion Sunday is this: Even though we can remove ourselves from situations, activities and relationships which lead us into sinful deed, we cannot remove the sinful nature from our lives. This is simply a fact of fallen humanity. We were born with and will continue to struggle with our tendency to rebel against God and our desire to follow our will instead of his. No matter how devoted to Christ we are . . . no matter how serious we are in striving for spiritual growth . . . no matter how much we pray and read the Bible . . . no matter how many situations, relationships and activities we remove ourselves from, our sinful nature will manifest itself in our thoughts, words and deeds. But God will not let our sins, failures and shortcomings defeat us! He has provided us with a wonderful opportunity to dine with him and share with him all the ways we have failed to live up to his expectations.

In Holy Communion, we kneel with humble hearts in the presence of our King and we confess to him that we have failed to be faithful to him and loving to our neighbor. We tell him that we have tried . . . but somehow the old sinful nature took control. And then, if we are genuinely repentant and sorry for our sins, God does not angrily fuss or threaten us with punishment. He says, "My child, I know you have tried. Your sinful nature is powerful. I have forgiven you. Now let me strengthen you for tomorrow." You see, Christ wants to forgive you of your past sins and strengthen you for your future struggle with your sinful nature. Today he wants to free you from the weight of those sins which plague your life and pull you down like a dragging anchor. But for you to realize your freedom from those sins, to realize that he has truly forgiven you, you must also forgive yourself!

In a few minutes, you will be invited to bring your sins to this Altar, confess them painfully and honestly to God and then leave them there! Do not pick them back up again! For in Micah 7:19 we read that when we confess our sins to God, he casts them into the depths of the sea. And that's where they remain. They're gone!

I once read about a missionary named George Woodall, who used that verse from Micah in a unique way. When a person came to him and said she was worried if God had really forgiven her for a certain sin, he said, "I think God would tell you to mind your own business!" When she questioned what he meant, he replied, "It's God's business to say when he has forgiven you, not yours. And he said he has thrown your sin into the depths of the sea and at that very spot he has posted a sign just for you which says, 'No Fishing'." She got the point and was relieved.

I hope you will be as relieved when you rise from the Lord's Table this morning. Regardless of how awful you consider your sin to be, no matter how ugly and unforgiveable you think it is, be reminded, in the bread and wine, of his enormous love for you. Be reminded that he has indeed forgiven you and cast your sins into the depths of the sea and he wants you to leave them there. Don't go fishing for them — don't dredge them up again. If God Almighty has declared you forgiven — you are forgiven indeed! That's all there is to it.

So we've seen this morning that we cannot run away from the stench of sin. It permeates all we do, say and think, because it is a part of our Fallen Nature. But there are two things we can do about the manifestations of sin in our daily lives: First, we can know our weaknesses and avoid those situations, relationships and activities which lead us into sinful actions. Second, we can confess our sins to God with repentant hearts in the confidence that he will forgive us and we will be free to live anew! We no longer have to run from sin for the Lord has a way for us to deal with it! Isn't it good to be a Child of God?!

www.ingramcontent.com/pod-product-compliance
Lightning Source LLC
Chambersburg PA
CBHW071742040426
42446CB00012B/2437